A Guide to
AMERICAN STATES

South Dakota

THE MOUNT RUSHMORE STATE

MEDIA ENHANCED BOOKS
AV2
BY WEIGL
ADDED VALUE · AUDIO VISUAL

www.av2books.com

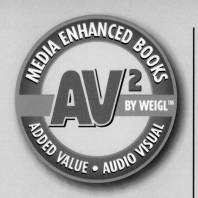

MEDIA ENHANCED BOOKS
AV²
BY WEIGL™
ADDED VALUE · AUDIO VISUAL

AV² provides enriched content that supplements and complements this book. Weigl's AV² books strive to create inspired learning and engage young minds in a total learning experience.

Your AV² Media Enhanced books come alive with...

Audio
Listen to sections of the book read aloud.

Key Words
Study vocabulary, and complete a matching word activity.

Video
Watch informative video clips.

Quizzes
Test your knowledge.

Embedded Weblinks
Gain additional information for research.

Slide Show
View images and captions, and prepare a presentation.

Try This!
Complete activities and hands-on experiments.

... and much, much more!

Go to **www.av2books.com,** and enter this book's unique code.

BOOK CODE

A588604

AV² by Weigl brings you media enhanced books that support active learning.

Published by AV² by Weigl
350 5ᵗʰ Avenue, 59ᵗʰ Floor
New York, NY 10118
Website: www.av2books.com   www.weigl.com

Library of Congress Cataloging-in-Publication Data

Strudwick, Leslie, 1970-
 South Dakota / Leslie Strudwick.
   p. cm. -- (A guide to American states)
 Includes index.
 ISBN 978-1-61690-814-0 (hardcover : alk. paper) -- ISBN 978-1-61690-490-6 (online)
 1. South Dakota--Juvenile literature. I. Title.
 F651.3.S77 2011
 978.3--dc23
                         2011019024

Printed in the United States of America in North Mankato, Minnesota
2 3 4 5 6 7 8 9 0 19 18 17 16 15

102015
300915

Project Coordinator Jordan McGill
Art Director Terry Paulhus

Photo Credits
Every reasonable effort has been made to trace ownership and to obtain permission to reprint copyright material. The publishers would be pleased to have any errors or omissions brought to their attention so that they may be corrected in subsequent printings.

Weigl acknowledges Getty Images as its primary image supplier for this title.

Contents

In the Black Hills granite outcroppings have resisted erosion, forming tall granite pillars known as The Needles.

Introduction

T he state of South Dakota sweeps from the Black Hills to the Great Plains. In the region called the Badlands, time and weather have carved the rock into forms that seem like something from another planet. On the plains, the line between land and sky stretches as far as can be seen.

South Dakotans cherish their land and treasure their state's strong American Indian culture. They celebrate the settlers of European **heritage** who turned the plains into productive farmland. They look to the pioneers' work ethic for inspiration. South Dakotans are proud of their farming communities and their cities' industries.

South Dakota is mostly grassland. Forests cover only about 4 percent of the state.

It took 14 years to create Mount Rushmore. Work on the memorial began in 1927 and ended in 1941. The sculptor started with George Washington.

South Dakota is known as the Mount Rushmore State because it is home to the national memorial Mount Rushmore. Carved into a Black Hills mountainside is a massive sculpture that **commemorates** four important U.S. presidents. The sculpture shows the faces of George Washington, Thomas Jefferson, Theodore Roosevelt, and Abraham Lincoln. They represent the birth of the United States, its political struggles, and its path to freedom and democracy.

South Dakota is also called the Sunshine State, for its bright sunny days, and the Coyote State, for its wildlife. Visitors can see historic sites and view natural wonders. They learn that South Dakota is at the center of the United States, in more ways than one.

Where Is South Dakota?

South Dakota is part of the Great Plains region of the United States. The states of Minnesota and Iowa are across the border to the east. North Dakota lies to the north, Nebraska is to the south, and Wyoming and Montana are to the west. The geographic center of the United States is in South Dakota, about 20 miles north of the city of Belle Fourche. The spot was designated in 1959, when Alaska and Hawai'i became states.

Custer State Park has 71,000 acres of land. The park's scenic drives include Needles Highway, which takes visitors through the granite pillars.

Millions of tourists visit South Dakota each year. Mount Rushmore National Memorial is one of many destinations. Custer State Park, in the Black Hills, attracts wildlife enthusiasts. A herd of 1,300 bison roams the parkland. Visitors who take vehicles on Wildlife Loop Road are often stopped by bison that are crossing the pavement.

Travelers take road trips to see the eerie rock formations in the Badlands. Outdoor lovers camp, fish, and hike. Many people explore the nation's **frontier** past by visiting historical sites.

The states' pioneer days were a time of both promise and conflict. There were many clashes over territory between settlers of European descent and the American Indians. Miners swarmed the Black Hills, panning for gold. Rowdy and lawless towns, such as Deadwood, sprang up. This rich and colorful history brings many people to South Dakota, so they can see the landscape and historic places for themselves.

I DIDN'T KNOW THAT!

South Dakota has a land area of approximately 75,885 square miles.

The state's highest point is Harney Peak in the Black Hills. It is 7,242 feet above sea level.

The Missouri River runs from north to south, cutting the state in two.

The state slogan is "Great Faces. Great Places." This refers to the Mount Rushmore monument and also to the interesting people and places across the state. The slogan appears on license plates and some road signs.

Each fall, the state hires riders to round up the bison in Custer State Park. The state typically receives over 100 applications from would-be buckaroos.

Mapping South Dakota

The South Dakota transportation system includes more than 82,000 miles of highways, roads, and streets. Travelers can drive to South Dakota on interstate highways. Interstate 90 and I-190 run east-west. I-29 runs north-south in the eastern part of the state. Nine highway bridges cross the Missouri River. The largest airports are in Aberdeen, Pierre, Rapid City, Sioux Falls, and Watertown.

Sites and Symbols

STATE SEAL
South Dakota

STATE BIRD
Chinese Ring-necked Pheasant

STATE FLOWER
American Pasqueflower

STATE FLAG
South Dakota

STATE ANIMAL
Coyote

STATE TREE
Black Hills Spruce

Nickname Mount Rushmore State, Sunshine State, Coyote State, Artesian State, Blizzard State

Motto Under God, the People Rule

Song "Hail, South Dakota" words and music by Deecort Hammitt

Entered the Union November 2, 1889, as the 40th state

Capital Pierre

Population (2010 Census) 814,180 Ranked 46th state

Map labels (South Dakota map):

MONTANA

NORTH DAKOTA

MINNESOTA

WYOMING

SOUTH DAKOTA

IOWA

NEBRASKA

Bowman · Scranton · Strasburg · Monango · Oakes · Hankinson
Haynes
Morristown · McLaughlin · Herreid · Frederick · Sisseton · Peever
Buffalo · Mobridge · Selby · Bowdle · Ipswich · Webster · Marvin · Milbank
Dupree · Mellette · Madison
Eagle Butte · Redfield · Watertown · Canby
Belle Fourche · Agar
Spearfish · Blunt · Wessington · De Smet
Sturgis · Pierre · Huron · Brookings
Lead · Carthage · Madison · Flandreau
Rapid City · Box Elder · Philip · Midland · Dell Rapids · Humboldt
Wall · Draper · Presho · Chamberlain · Mitchell · Luverne
Custer · Belvidere · Stickney · Dolton · Sioux Falls
Hot Springs · Winner · Ravinia
Oelrichs · Martin · Mission · Burke · Yankton
Pine Ridge · Batesland · Cody · Valentine · Spencer · Vermillion
Chadron · Gordon · Ainsworth · Bassett · O Neill · Sioux City
Harrison · Clearwater
Alliance · Norfolk

Map Scale
0 ——————————— 100 Miles

N

STATE CAPITAL

When South Dakota became a state in 1889, Pierre was selected as a temporary capital because it is in the center of the state. Over the next few years, other towns challenged Pierre to become the capital, although none of these challenges was successful. In 1904, the state legislature voted Pierre the permanent capital and began work on a **capitol**. The building was finished in 1910.

United States

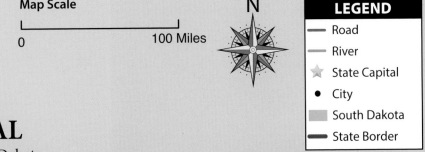

Hawai'i   Alaska

South Dakota

The Land

The Black Hills extend from South Dakota's western edge into Wyoming. The land rises to more than 7,200 feet above sea level. The rugged Black Hills region includes deep valleys and densely forested slopes. From a distance the hills' wooded slopes look almost black, giving them their name.

The dry hills and valleys of the Great Plains cover the rest of the western part of the state. The **eroded** rock formations of the Badlands are found in this area. The Eastern Prairie covers the eastern part of the state. This area is characterized by low, rolling hills. It offers plenty of grazing space and the most **fertile** farmland in the state.

BLACK HILLS

The 1.2 million acres of Black Hills National Forest include more than 450 miles of trails.

FARMLAND

South Dakota has more than 550 different types of soils. The rich Houdek soil of the Eastern Prairie was declared the official state soil in 1990.

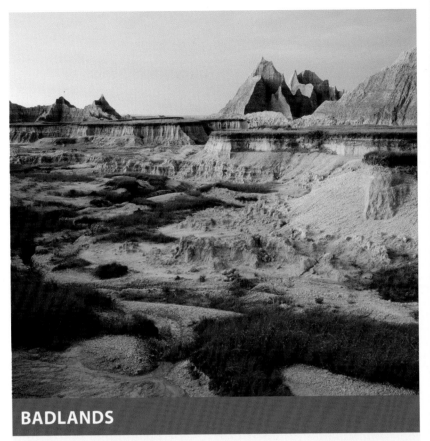

BADLANDS

The Badlands Wilderness Area in Badlands National Park stretches across 64,000 acres.

MISSOURI RIVER

Excluding the rivers in the northeast corner, all of South Dakota's rivers flow into the Missouri River. These include the Big Sioux, Vermillion, James, and Grand Rivers.

South Dakota has so many streams and lakes, it has more shoreline than the state of Florida does.

Human-made Sylvan Lake is called the "crown jewel" of Custer State Park.

Some of the natural features in South Dakota were created by massive blocks of moving ice called glaciers. These glaciers once covered the land. When the glaciers **receded**, they created streams. The waterways cut sharp valleys through the **till** left behind. Chunks of glacial ice also formed the many lakes of the northeastern part of the state.

Black Hills National Forest has 450 miles of hiking trails and 1,300 miles of streams.

Because of the temperature extremes in South Dakota, the U.S. government studied ice forces on the state's bridges over a six-year period. This included one of the state's mildest winters and one of its coldest winters. Researchers looked at ice thickness in the water below the bridges. They studied wind conditions and other related factors. They are using their findings to improve future bridge designs.

Climate

Rain falls mostly from April to September, with higher rainfall occurring east of the Missouri River. Temperatures in South Dakota vary greatly throughout the year. For example, the average January temperature in Sioux Falls is 14° Fahrenheit. In July the average temperature is 73° F. The record high temperature, 120° F, was set in Gann Valley on July 5, 1936. This astounding high was matched at Usta on July 15, 2006. The lowest recorded temperature is −58° F, set on February 17, 1936, at McIntosh.

Average Annual Temperatures Across South Dakota

South Dakota's temperatures cover a wide range in the course of a year. However, the average annual temperatures recorded at different places around the state tend to be similar. What aspects of the state's geography account for this similarity?

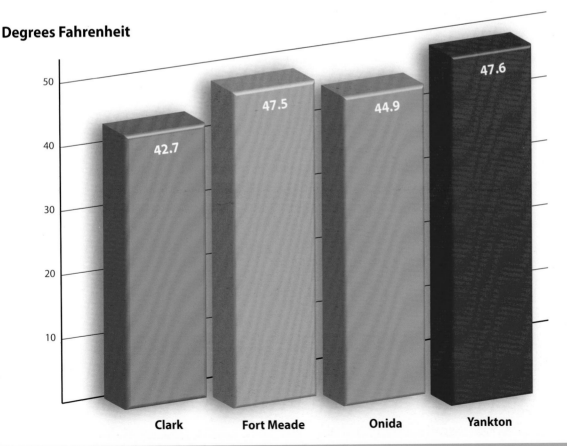

Degrees Fahrenheit

Clark	Fort Meade	Onida	Yankton
42.7	47.5	44.9	47.6

Natural Resources

The state seal is a symbol that represents some of the state's more important natural resources. The seal features a farmer plowing his fields. It shows a steamboat chugging down a river. It pictures cattle as they graze. There is also a **smelting** furnace, which represents mining. The soil, water, grasses, and minerals have long been vital to the success of South Dakotans.

The flow of water on the Missouri River is controlled by dams, which create water reservoirs and generate electricity. The dams on the Missouri River in South Dakota are federally operated. They are managed by the U.S. Army Corps of Engineers.

South Dakota's fertile farmland is one of its most important natural resources. The nutrient-rich soil supports and nourishes crops, including corn and wheat. Many areas are left unplanted so that livestock can feed on the wild grasses. Beneath the soil and on the hillsides, minerals such as gold, quartzite, limestone, and gypsum can be found.

Water is another valuable resource in the state. Water nurtures wildlife, supports the fishing industry, and is used as an energy source to generate electricity. South Dakotans use more electricity from **hydroelectric** power plants than from any other source. Four of South Dakota's hydroelectric power plants are located on the Missouri River.

Most of the state's gold was taken from the Homestake mine in Lead until the mine closed in 2002. However, there are still many open-pit mines in operation.

Plants

In South Dakota, the native trees include elm, ash, cottonwood, and aspen. Water-loving cottonwoods grow along the Missouri and other rivers. However, most of the state's trees are in the Black Hills National Forest. In these woods, birch, juniper, spruce, and ponderosa pine trees are plentiful. Evergreens make up the great majority of the trees in the Black Hills National Forest.

There are far more varieties of flowers and grasses in South Dakota than there are trees. Roses, poppies, and sunflowers are scattered on the prairies, along with wild orange geraniums, goldenrods, and black-eyed Susans. Prickly cacti and yucca plants grow in the drier western portion of the state. Some of the flowers found in the shady Black Hills include colorful mariposa lilies, forget-me-nots, lady slippers, bluebells, and larkspurs.

AMERICAN PASQUE

The pasque is related to the buttercup. Because its blooms are one of the first signs of spring in South Dakota and neighboring states, it is also known as the May Day Flower.

COTTONWOOD

In fall, the state's cottonwood trees turn bright gold. Mature cottonwood trees take in up to 200 gallons of water per day.

BIG BLUESTEM GRASS

Native to the state, big bluestem grows from 4 to 7 feet tall. It is called the monarch of the prairie grasses.

QUAKING ASPEN

Quaking aspen trees have one of the widest distributions of trees in North America. They are often found in areas between grasslands and evergreens and grow well in the Black Hills.

The Lakota Sioux Indians called the pasque flower *hosi' cepka*, which means "child's navel." The flower looks like a baby's bellybutton.

Lakota children have a game that they play with needlethread grass. It involves throwing the grass heads at one another to see the grass stick to clothing and hair.

Buffalo grass has stems that run above the ground, similar to the way strawberry plants have runners. The stems help the grass form thick mats on the ground.

The Black Hills spruce is a type of white pine that grows slowly and can stand up to the strong winter winds in the Black Hills.

Animals

The coyote, which is the state animal, roams throughout South Dakota, though its numbers are decreasing. It is mostly **nocturnal** and hunts alone or in packs. This animal can run quickly, at speeds of up to 40 miles per hour. Coyotes are most numerous along the Missouri River and in the Black Hills, but they also make their homes on the prairies. White-tailed deer, antelope, beavers, foxes, bobcats, raccoons, and porcupines also live in the state.

South Dakota's rivers and lakes are teeming with fish. Some of the fish in the state's waters include walleye, perch, northern pike, sturgeon, trout, and catfish. Bird-watchers stay on the lookout for bald eagles and golden eagles. Canada geese are plentiful, especially during their winter migration. The state is also home to western meadowlarks, American goldfinches, northern flickers, and brown thrashers. Ground-nesting birds include wild turkeys, sage grouse, sharp-tailed grouse, and Chinese ring-necked pheasants.

MULE DEER

In the Badlands, mule deer are more common that white-tailed deer. These creatures get their name from their mule-like ears.

BALD EAGLE

Bald eagles are found near rivers and other waterways because they like to eat fish. The birds' nests are called eyries or aeries.

BOBCAT

The bobcat inhabits remote areas, such as the Black Hills. These animals are most active at twilight.

BLACK-FOOTED FERRET

The black-footed ferret is the only ferret native to North America. It was considered endangered by the U.S. government, but it has been re-introduced to South Dakota, and its numbers are climbing.

The state insect is the honeybee. South Dakota is a national leader in honey production.

Porcupines are heavyset rodents that wake up at dusk to look for food. At dawn they go to sleep in hollow logs and other "found" structures. They usually live alone and do not build nests.

Tourism

Tourism is an important part of South Dakota's economy. The Badlands and the Black Hills draw millions of tourists every year to its parks and historical sites. Many visitors want to see the land of the Sioux and the sites of major clashes between American Indians and white settlers.

Mount Rushmore National Memorial is in the Black Hills. It has been called the Shrine of Democracy. About 2 million people visit the memorial each year. The faces of George Washington, Thomas Jefferson, Theodore Roosevelt, and Abraham Lincoln are carved into the granite on the mountainside. Mount Rushmore is one of the largest sculptures in the world. Nearby, another mountainside sculpture is under construction. A massive sculpture of the Lakota Sioux chief Crazy Horse has been taking shape since the 1940s.

PALISADES

The quartzite rock cliffs in Palisades State Park are ancient. The 50-foot-high cliffs are thought to be 1.2 billion years old.

CRAZY HORSE MEMORIAL

A sculptor named Korczak Ziolkowski and a Lakota chief named Henry Standing Bear started work on the sculpture in 1948. The sculptor's family has continued the nonprofit project, under the guidance of a board of directors.

DEADWOOD

The former mining town of Deadwood now features gambling halls. Tourists can visit the graves of Wild West legends such as Wild Bill Hickok and Calamity Jane.

DINOSAUR PARK

Life-sized dinosaur replicas fill the park. Scientists have found bones from three-toed horses, saber-toothed cats, and dinosaurs such as the *Apatosaurus* in the state. Tourists can tour the dinosaur fossil beds.

The faces on Mount Rushmore stand about 60 feet high from forehead to chin. Presidents Washington, Jefferson, Roosevelt, and Lincoln were meant to stand for certain ideals. These ideals are, in order, independence, democratic process, world leadership, and equality.

Since 1890 visitors have gone to the town of Hot Springs to splash in its large indoor swimming pool, which is fed by a natural spring. Long before the indoor pool opened, American Indians were visiting the warm mineral springs for their healing properties.

Visitors to South Dakota can see the grave and memorial of Sioux leader Sitting Bull. It is located on a bluff overlooking the Missouri River in the northern part of the state.

Industry

N ine-tenths of South Dakota's land is devoted to farming and ranching. Among the crops commonly grown in South Dakota are corn, soybeans, wheat, and sunflowers. South Dakota farmers raise cattle, pigs, sheep, and poultry.

Industries in South Dakota
Value of Goods and Services in Millions of Dollars

South Dakota celebrates the pioneer spirit of the early South Dakotans, who were farmers, trappers, and miners. Today, however, much of the pioneering is done in service industries, such as government services, financial services, and tourism. How are these newer growth industries tied to those that dominated in the past?

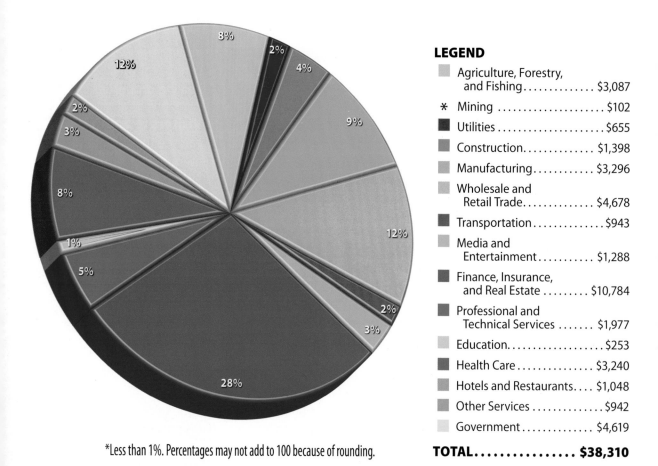

LEGEND

	Agriculture, Forestry, and Fishing	$3,087
*	Mining	$102
	Utilities	$655
	Construction	$1,398
	Manufacturing	$3,296
	Wholesale and Retail Trade	$4,678
	Transportation	$943
	Media and Entertainment	$1,288
	Finance, Insurance, and Real Estate	$10,784
	Professional and Technical Services	$1,977
	Education	$253
	Health Care	$3,240
	Hotels and Restaurants	$1,048
	Other Services	$942
	Government	$4,619

*Less than 1%. Percentages may not add to 100 because of rounding.

TOTAL $38,310

Other key industries include mining, manufacturing, and hydroelectric power. The majority of the state's mining income comes from construction materials such as cement, granite, crushed stone, sand, and gravel.

Agriculture, mining, utilities, construction, and manufacturing account for about a quarter of the state's total economy. However, the majority of industries that drive South Dakota's economy today are service industries. These are businesses in which what is "produced" is a service, such as a **financial** services or health care.

Spring wheat is mainly grown in the northern part of the state. Winter wheat is grown in the south-central area.

Goods and Services

The service sector, which includes health care and education, employs more South Dakotans than any other part of the economy. Most service-sector businesses are located in the state's largest cities. Sioux Falls is South Dakota's financial center. Most banking companies in the state have their main offices there, as do insurance and real estate companies.

Daktronics is a leading manufacturer of scoreboards. The company is located in Brookings.

Wild Water West is a popular waterpark in Sioux Falls. Most jobs there are summer jobs, but the paintball area can be reserved in other seasons.

Manufacturing is still important to the state's economy, however. Industrial machinery, food products, computers, consumer electronics, and office equipment are all made in the Mount Rushmore State.

South Dakota's agricultural products support its food processing industry. Cattle, pigs, and poultry go into the production of meat and meat products. Sioux Falls has the largest meat-processing plant in the state. It also has a large dairy-processing plant. Other food-processing activities in South Dakota include flour milling and baking.

The time it takes, on average, for South Dakotans to get to work ranks among the lowest in the nation. In recent years, the average commute has been just over 16 minutes.

Among the 25 largest business establishments in the state, those with more than 3,000 employees include John Morrel & Co., Sanford Health, Avera McKennan Hospital, Citigroup, and Wells Fargo. All are in Sioux Falls.

John Morrel & Co. makes meat products, such as bacon and pepperoni. The company's brands include Eckrich and Armour. Its largest facility is in Sioux Falls.

The public school system is one of the state's leading employers. South Dakota is ranked among the top states in the nation when comparing the number of students to the number of school computers.

American Indians

Prehistoric humans lived in the South Dakota area as far back as 10,000 years ago. These early peoples hunted mammoths and other large animals. They trapped and speared bison, also known as buffalo.

Around the year 200, a group known as the Mound Builders settled east of the Missouri along what is now called the Big Sioux River. These people built huge dome-shaped mounds of earth for burials and other ceremonial purposes. Sometime around the year 1000, the Mound Builders stopped making their great earthworks. They seemed to disappear.

The American Indians used all parts of the bison they hunted. Among many uses, the hides became material for clothing and hair was made into rope. Bones were used for weapons and tools. The hooves were boiled to make glue.

By the time European explorers arrived in the area in the 1700s, several American Indian groups were living on the land, each with its own culture. The Mandan and the Arikara lived in settled farming villages along the Missouri River. They built round houses of earth and raised corn, beans, and squash. Both groups traded with hunting peoples from the Great Plains to the west.

The Cheyenne, the Crow, and the Pawnee exchanged bison hides and meat as well as horses with the people along the Missouri. In the 1700s, the nomadic people known as the Sioux followed bison herds into the region. They eventually occupied a wide area centered on the Black Hills, pushing other tribes out.

Different groups of Sioux called themselves the Nakota, Lakota, or Dakota. Dakota means "friends" or "allies."

Lewis and Clark traveled through what is now South Dakota in 1804. On September 7, they saw prairie dogs for the first time. The members of the expedition tried to capture one to ship back home for show.

Explorers

I n 1682, René-Robert Cavelier, sieur de La Salle, claimed all the land drained by the Mississippi River for France. The French territory was named Louisiana, and it included what is now South Dakota.

Although French fur traders traveled near the area earlier, the first European explorations of South Dakota did not occur until the 1740s. That is when François and Louis Joseph de La Vérendrye followed the Missouri River, looking for a water route to the Pacific Ocean. The brothers did not find the ocean, but they did open the Upper Missouri Valley to the French fur trade.

France turned over control of the Louisiana region to Spain in 1762, but the land returned to French control in 1800. In 1803, the United States acquired the land from France in the Louisiana Purchase. At that time, South Dakota was still mostly unexplored by non-Indians, so President Thomas Jefferson sent Meriwether Lewis and William Clark to study the region. After the Lewis and Clark **expedition**, more fur traders moved to the area along the Missouri River. In 1817 the first permanent settlement by people of European descent was built at the site of present-day Fort Pierre.

Timeline of Settlement

Early Explorers and Traders

1743 Brothers François and Louis Joseph de La Vérendrye reach what is now South Dakota, on their trip up the Missouri River.

1785 Around this time, French fur trader Pierre Dorion arrives in the region from Canada. He marries a Sioux woman.

1790s French-Canadians travel southwest into the region. British fur traders follow the Missouri River into the region. They make trades for buffalo, beaver, and other furs.

1804 Meriwether Lewis and William Clark meet Dorion while traveling on the Missouri. Dorion serves as an interpreter, helping the explorers talk with American Indians in the region.

First Settlements

1808 Manuel Lisa establishes the Missouri Fur Company, which begins building trading posts along the Missouri River.

1811 Traders explore the Black Hills region. Soon the James River and Big Sioux River have trading posts, too.

1817 Joseph La Framboise builds Fort Teton at the site of Fort Pierre.

1824 Gabriel Renville is born at Big Stone Lake to fur-trading parents of mixed European and American Indian ancestry. He eventually becomes leader of a Sioux group and teaches members of the group to farm.

1855 John B. S. Todd arrives and starts a trading post for soldiers at Fort Randall. He starts selling land as well. In 1861, he travels to Washington, D.C., to try to convince Congress to declare the area a U.S. territory.

Territory and Statehood

1861 The Dakota Territory is established. It includes large parts of Wyoming and Montana, along with present-day North and South Dakota.

1862 The Homestead Act is approved by Congress. The act awards up to 160 acres to those who improve the land by building a house and growing crops for a five-year period. Many settlers begin to arrive, including the family of Laura Ingalls Wilder, who goes on to write *Little House on the Prairie*.

1864 and 1868 Land that is now Wyoming and Montana is taken from the Dakota Territory.

1889 The remaining Dakota Territory is divided in two parts in February.

1889 North Dakota and South Dakota are admitted to the Union as separate states in November.

Early Settlers

By the 1850s the fur trade was ending and farming was becoming the new way of life for settlers in the region. In 1861 the Dakota Territory was organized. At first it included what is now North and South Dakota as well as large parts of Wyoming and Montana. As people began settling in the region and farming the land, towns such as Sioux Falls and Yankton were established.

Map of Settlements and Resources in Early South Dakota

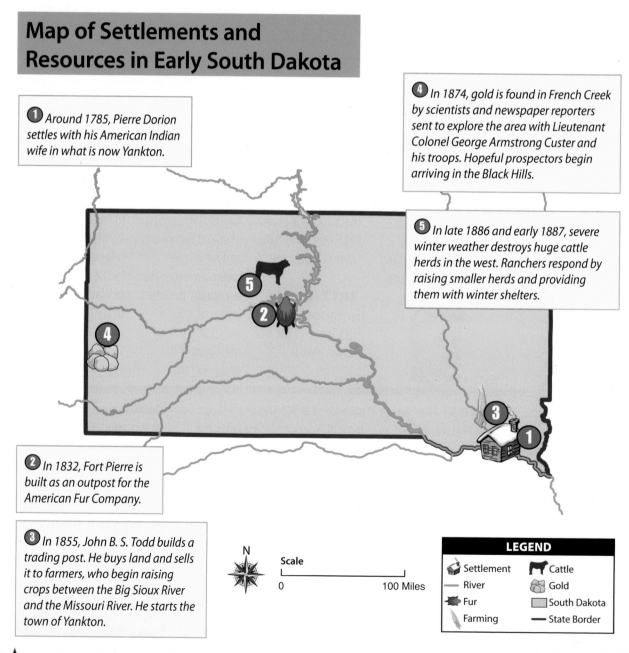

4 In 1874, gold is found in French Creek by scientists and newspaper reporters sent to explore the area with Lieutenant Colonel George Armstrong Custer and his troops. Hopeful prospectors begin arriving in the Black Hills.

1 Around 1785, Pierre Dorion settles with his American Indian wife in what is now Yankton.

5 In late 1886 and early 1887, severe winter weather destroys huge cattle herds in the west. Ranchers respond by raising smaller herds and providing them with winter shelters.

2 In 1832, Fort Pierre is built as an outpost for the American Fur Company.

3 In 1855, John B. S. Todd builds a trading post. He buys land and sells it to farmers, who begin raising crops between the Big Sioux River and the Missouri River. He starts the town of Yankton.

N

Scale

0   100 Miles

LEGEND

Settlement		Cattle	
River		Gold	
Fur		South Dakota	
Farming		State Border	

The U.S. government pressured the Sioux to give up some of the land they lived on. In return for their land, the government promised food, education, and health care. The Sioux were moved to new lands called **reservations**. However, in 1874 gold was discovered on a Black Hills Sioux reservation, and thousands of miners flocked to the area. After years of battling to stay on the land, the Sioux were forced to give up even more land to the newcomers.

While miners were rushing to the Black Hills, many Americans from the East and European **immigrants** headed for the prairies of eastern South Dakota. The first railroad reached the area in 1873, after which thousands of new farmers and ranchers came to the Dakota Territory. This period was called the "Great Dakota Boom." Russians, Swedes, Germans, and Czechs were just some of the immigrant groups who grew crops on land that was once considered unsuitable for farming.

In 1890, U.S. troops entered a Lakota camp on the Lakota Pine Ridge Indian Reservation to try to disarm the American Indians. The troops killed at least 150 men, women, and children. The Wounded Knee Massacre, as it has been called, is now marked by a national monument.

I DIDN'T KNOW THAT!

Brothers François and Louis Joseph de La Vérendrye buried a "lead tablet" on their way back down the Missouri. The tablet claimed the land for France. It was not discovered until 1913, when some Fort Pierre high school students found it.

The Sioux considered the Black Hills their sacred ancestral home. In 1875 the U.S. government offered Sioux Indian groups $6 million to vacate the hills, but they refused. The federal government eventually seized the Black Hills. This led to the Sioux War of 1876, during which U.S. Army Lieutenant Colonel George Armstrong Custer was defeated in the Battle of the Little Bighorn.

In the heart of the Badlands, visitors can tour the site of the Wounded Knee massacre, where hundreds of Lakota Sioux were slain by the U.S. Army in 1890.

In 1980 the U.S. Supreme Court ordered the federal government to pay $105 million to the Sioux for Black Hills land that had been taken in the 1870s.

Notable People

Prominent people from South Dakota have shaped U.S. history. Various South Dakotans have served the nation as politicians and in the military. Many have been important in business and education. Many South Dakotans who participated in the state's development also made contributions to the nation's progress.

BENJAMIN REIFEL
(1906–1990)

Born in a log cabin on the Rosebud Indian Reservation, Benjamin Reifel attended South Dakota State College. In 1932, he was hired by the U.S. Department of the Interior. He worked in American Indian affairs until 1960, earning a Ph.D. from Harvard University in 1952. He was then elected to become a U.S. representative from South Dakota, the first American Indian from the state to serve in the U.S. Congress.

HUBERT HUMPHREY
(1911–1978)

Hubert Humphrey was born in Wallace and raised in Doland. He became a U.S. senator for Minnesota in 1949 and U.S. vice president, serving with President Lyndon Johnson, beginning in 1965. First trained as a pharmacist, Humphrey became a political science professor, worked as a news commentator, and served as the mayor of Minneapolis before arriving on the national political stage. In 1980, two years after his death, he was awarded the Presidential Medal of Freedom.

JOSEPH FOSS
(1915–2003)

After graduating from the University of South Dakota, Joseph Foss enlisted in the U.S. Marine Corps. He was given the Congressional Medal of Honor for bravery during his military service as a pilot in World War II. In South Dakota, he was twice elected governor. Foss was the first commissioner of the American Football League.

GEORGE MCGOVERN
(1922–)

George McGovern was born on a farm in South Dakota. He served in the U.S. Army Air Corps in World War II then returned to the state for college. He was a professor of history and government before serving in the U.S. House of Representatives for two terms. He was in the U.S. Senate from 1963 to 1981.

BILLY MILLS
(1938–)

A member of the Lakota Sioux and the U.S. Marines, Billy Mills was born on the Pine Ridge Indian Reservation. At the 1964 Olympics, he arrived as an unknown and won the gold medal in the 10,000-meter race, a first for an American. He later became active in American Indian affairs. The film *Running Brave* is based on his life.

I DIDN'T KNOW THAT!

Tom Brokaw (1940–) was born in Webster and graduated from the University of South Dakota. He started his TV news career in Iowa and ultimately served as the *Today Show* host and then evening news anchor for NBC-TV. He continues to host news specials for the network.

Tom Daschle (1947–) is from Aberdeen. He graduated from South Dakota State University and joined the U.S. Air Force. Daschle was then elected to the U.S. House of Representatives, representing South Dakota from 1979 to 1987. He then was elected to the U.S. Senate, serving from 1987 to 2005.

Population

U nlike many states, South Dakota does not have a large number of major urban centers. Half of the state's residents live in relatively small cities and towns, and the other half live in rural areas. The largest city in the state is Sioux Falls, with about 158,000 people. The more heavily populated towns are east of the Missouri River, centered in the best farming regions. In the western part of the state, most of the people live around the Black Hills, the site of many mining communities. About 98 percent of all South Dakotans were born in the United States. Large numbers of them claim German, Scandinavian, Irish, British, Czech, Dutch, or American Indian heritage.

South Dakota Population 1950–2010

South Dakota's population has increased in most decades since 1950, but the most dramatic population growth has been in the past twenty years. What do you think is contributing to the recent population growth?

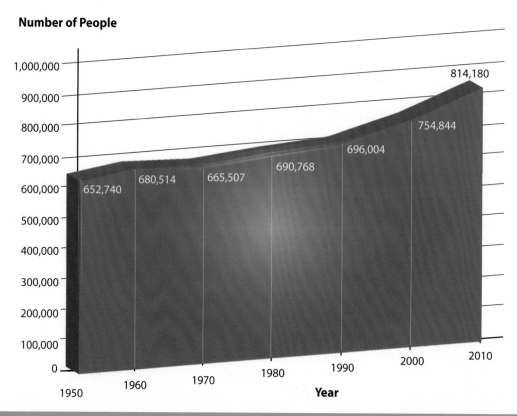

Number of People

814,180
754,844
696,004
690,768
665,507
680,514
652,740

1,000,000
900,000
800,000
700,000
600,000
500,000
400,000
300,000
200,000
100,000
0

1950 1960 1970 1980 1990 2000 2010

Year

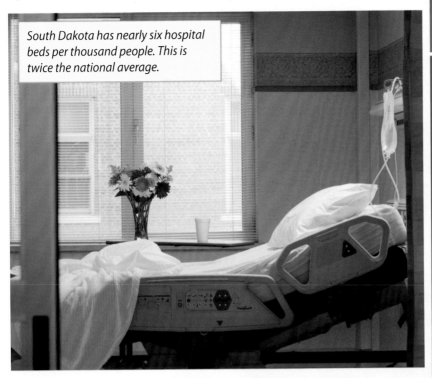

South Dakota has nearly six hospital beds per thousand people. This is twice the national average.

Today, South Dakota ranks 46th among the 50 states in total population.

The 2010 Census found that the state's population had increased by 7.9 percent since the year 2000. The national population increase was 9.7 percent.

In South Dakota, there are nearly 11 people per square mile. This compares with the national average of about 87 people per square mile.

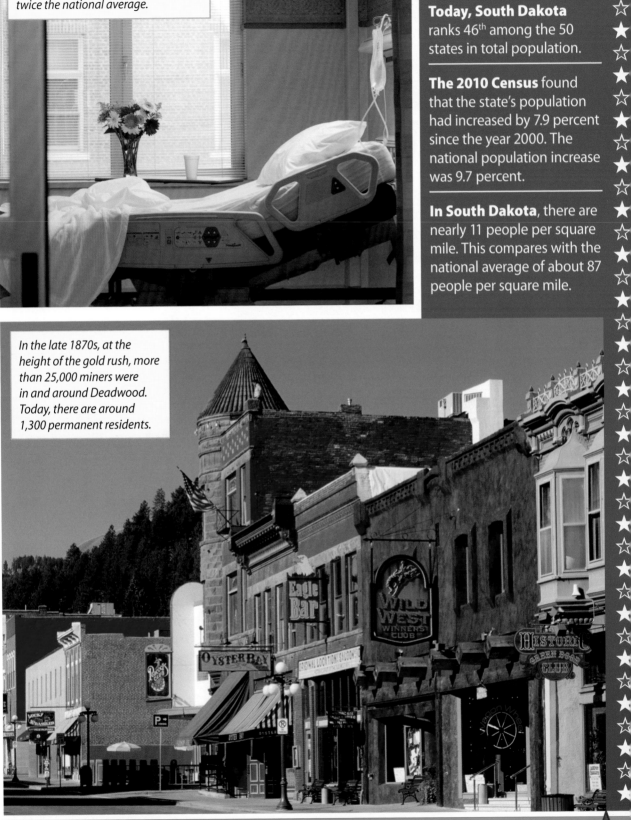

In the late 1870s, at the height of the gold rush, more than 25,000 miners were in and around Deadwood. Today, there are around 1,300 permanent residents.

The state legislature meets in the capitol for one short session each year. The regular session starts on the second Tuesday in January and lasts for 40 days. Legislators meet at other times if called by the governor.

Politics and Government

The government of South Dakota is divided into three parts. They are the executive, the legislative, and the judicial branches. The executive branch is headed by the governor, who is elected to a four-year term and can serve a maximum of two terms. Other key members of the executive branch include the lieutenant governor, the attorney general, the secretary of state, the commissioner of school and public lands, the treasurer, and the auditor.

The legislative branch of government consists of the 35-member Senate and the 70-member House of Representatives. One senator and two representatives are elected to two-year terms from each of the state's 35 legislative districts. The state court system is the judicial branch. The highest court is the five-judge state Supreme Court. Below it is the circuit court, followed by the magistrate courts. The judges are elected by the public.

In South Dakota, the costs of education, from kindergarten through college, account for nearly half of the state budget.

Cultural Groups

Many of the European settlers who came to South Dakota were of German heritage. Today German culture is still strong in the state. The largest group of non-European people in South Dakota is American Indians. They make up nearly 9 percent of the population. Other minority groups in South Dakota, including Hispanic Americans, Asian Americans, and African Americans, are quite small.

American Indian culture in South Dakota is evident throughout the state. On and off reservations, American Indians preserve traditional ways of life, from their arts and crafts to their cultural values. Large **powwows** are held throughout the year. At these celebratory gatherings, American Indians dress in traditional clothing. They sing, beat drums, dance, and celebrate their heritage. The people compete in dance contests, such as jingle and hoop dances, and raise money for American Indian scholarship funds.

The Dakota Sioux phrase how kola *is the state greeting. It means, "Hello, friend."*

Many of the Germans who traveled to the Dakotas were Hutterites. Their descendants dress and live simply. Living this way is central to the group's beliefs.

Early pioneer culture is celebrated in South Dakota, too. Related fairs and festivals are held mainly in the summer months. Spectators can watch gun-handling demonstrations at the Fort Sisseton Historical Festival. There are logging competitions at the Heart of the Hills Celebration in Hill City. Visitors can also relive the gold rush period during Days of '76 in Deadwood. The annual festival features a famous rodeo. At Gold Discovery Days, in Custer, there are competitions that include a gold nugget hunt.

I DIDN'T KNOW THAT!

Most of the German immigrants in South Dakota came from Russia. In the 1760s, Germans were invited to Russia to develop farmland. In exchange they were given religious freedom and land. In the 1860s, those rights were taken back, and many Russian Germans moved to the United States.

The German immigrants were usually Hutterites or Mennonites. Both groups believe in simple living and **pacifism**. The Hutterites share property. The Mennonites own individual farms.

The immigrants who moved to South Dakota usually came as single families, but 300 Welsh immigrants settled Powell, in Edmunds County, together in 1883.

A group of African Americans formed Blair colony in Sully County in 1900.

Unlike the pioneers who settled in the Midwest, pioneers in the Great Plains did not have to clear the land of trees. However, the unpredictable weather on the plains created its own special challenges.

Arts and Entertainment

S outh Dakota's American Indian heritage is reflected in its arts. American Indian artists keep ancient traditions alive by continuing to produce beautiful beadwork, pottery, and featherwork. Some artists still use natural dyes to paint pictures on skins or clothing. Others use less traditional **mediums**, such as oil paints, to create images on canvas.

Because the Mitchell Corn Palace is adorned with real grains, it is sometimes called the World's Largest Birdfeeder.

Oscar Howe was one of the best-known American Indian artists. A Yanktonai Sioux born in South Dakota in 1915, Howe used traditional symbols in new ways to portray modern Sioux culture. He worked as an art professor at the University of South Dakota for many years. Some of his work is still displayed there. Art lovers can also view his paintings at the Mitchell Corn Palace or the Oscar Howe Art Center, both located in Mitchell.

Events and festivals throughout the year keep residents and visitors entertained. In winter, Aberdeen hosts the Snow Queen Festival. During summer, people have their pick of rodeos to attend, such as the Black Hills Roundup in Belle Fourche. This well-known rodeo has been in operation since 1918. Along with rodeo events, the roundup offers carnival rides, country-music performances, and barbecues. During the annual Potato Days, in Clark, contestants decorate potatoes for prizes. A wrestling contest is held in a large tub of mashed potatoes. These spud-themed events are so popular, they been drawing people since 1972.

American Indian beadwork is an ancient artistic tradition that further evolved with the introduction of glass beads from European traders.

Many of the state's communities have drama groups. The most famous play in the state is the Black Hills Passion Play. It is performed in an outdoor theater in Spearfish every summer. It dramatizes the biblical story of Jesus.

Sioux Falls is home to the South Dakota Symphony and the Sioux Empire Youth Orchestra.

Laura Ingalls Wilder, author of the *Little House* books about frontier life, lived in De Smet for many years. Four of her books are set there.

The Academy Award–winning film *Dances with Wolves*, starring Kevin Costner, was filmed in South Dakota. Costner is affiliated with Tatanka, an art exhibit near Deadwood that explains the story of bison. The centerpiece is a sculpture of 14 bronze bison and three American Indians on horseback.

Sports

Whether it is a hot summer afternoon or a snowy winter morning, South Dakotans enjoy a variety of activities in the great outdoors. The state's many lakes allow visitors and residents alike to enjoy water sports such as boating, fishing, swimming, and windsurfing. On dry land, there are plenty of trails for hiking and biking. In the Black Hills National Forest people can go horseback riding, rock climbing, and camping.

In the winter, snowmobiling is a popular activity, as are downhill and cross-country skiing. Terry Peak, Deer Mountain, and Great Bear have slopes for downhill skiers and snowboarders. Terry Peak has the nation's highest lift-served ski hill east of the Rocky Mountains. Deer Mountain lights trails for skiing at night.

South Dakota has about 500 official rock-climbing courses, with different degrees of difficulty. Experienced climbers also climb in areas that have not been plotted.

Every August, the streets of Sturgis fill with the sound of motorcyclists revving their engines. Approximately 600,000 people pass through the town during this annual event. Motorcyclists cruise Main Street and ride together through the highways of the Black Hills. Concerts and other activities round out the popular event.

South Dakota has two semiprofessional basketball teams. The Sioux Falls Skyforce and Rapid City's Dakota Wizards are both members of the NBA Development League, the training league for the National Basketball Association. The Sioux Falls Fighting Pheasants play minor league baseball in the American Association of Independent Professional Baseball. South Dakotans also cheer for teams at the state's universities. The University of South Dakota Coyotes and the South Dakota State Jackrabbits draw big crowds for a number of sports, including football, basketball, and baseball.

The Sioux Falls Skyforce plays at the Sioux Falls Arena. The team is a member of the American Conference.

National Averages Comparison

T he United States is a federal republic, consisting of fifty states and the District of Columbia. Alaska and Hawai'i are the only non-contiguous, or non-touching, states in the nation. Today, the United States of America is the third-largest country in the world in population. The United States Census Bureau takes a census, or count of all the people, every ten years. It also regularly collects other kinds of data about the population and the economy. How does South Dakota compare to the national average?

Comparison Chart

United States 2010 Census Data *	USA	Souh Dakota
Admission to Union	NA	November 2, 1889
Land Area (in square miles)	3,537,438.44	75,884.64
Population Total	308,745,538	814,180
Population Density (people per square mile)	87.28	10.73
Population Percentage Change (April 1, 2000, to April 1, 2010)	9.7%	7.9%
White Persons (percent)	72.4%	85.9%
Black Persons (percent)	12.6%	1.3%
American Indian and Alaska Native Persons (percent)	0.9%	8.8%
Asian Persons (percent)	4.8%	0.9%
Native Hawaiian and Other Pacific Islander Persons (percent)	0.2%	—
Some Other Race (percent)	6.2%	0.9%
Persons Reporting Two or More Races (percent)	2.9%	2.1%
Persons of Hispanic or Latino Origin (percent)	16.3%	2.7%
Not of Hispanic or Latino Origin (percent)	83.7%	97.3%
Median Household Income	$52,029	$46,244
Percentage of People Age 25 or Over Who Have Graduated from High School	80.4%	84.6%

*All figures are based on the 2010 United States Census, with the exception of the last two items. Percentages may not add to 100 because of rounding.

How to Improve My Community

Strong communities make strong states. Think about what features are important in your community. What do you value? Education? Health? Forests? Safety? Beautiful spaces? Government works to help citizens create ideal living conditions that are fair to all by providing services in communities. Consider what changes you could make in your community. How would they improve your state as a whole? Using this concept web as a guide, write a report that outlines the features you think are most important in your community and what improvements could be made. A strong state needs strong communities.

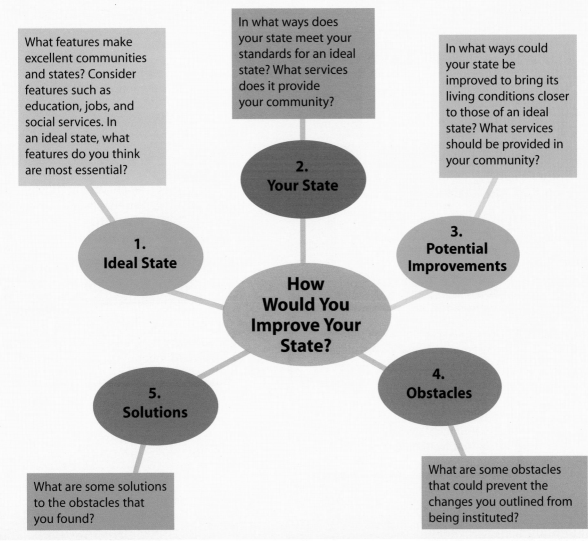

What features make excellent communities and states? Consider features such as education, jobs, and social services. In an ideal state, what features do you think are most essential?

In what ways does your state meet your standards for an ideal state? What services does it provide your community?

In what ways could your state be improved to bring its living conditions closer to those of an ideal state? What services should be provided in your community?

2. Your State

3. Potential Improvements

1. Ideal State

How Would You Improve Your State?

4. Obstacles

5. Solutions

What are some solutions to the obstacles that you found?

What are some obstacles that could prevent the changes you outlined from being instituted?

Exercise Your Mind!

Think about these questions and then use your research skills to find the answers and learn more fascinating facts about South Dakota. A teacher, librarian, or parent may be able to help you locate the best sources to use in your research.

1 One of South Dakota's many nicknames is the Artesian State, for the number of artesian wells in the area. What are artesian wells?

2 What famous host of a popular entertainment news program was born in South Dakota?

3 What important find was uncovered in the rocks of the Black Hills in 1990?

4 Where can you find more than 50 wax figures of people who played a role in South Dakota's history?

a. Miniature golf course
b. Tennis court
c. Amusement park
d. Indoor swimming pool

5 Calamity Jane is buried in Deadwood. What was Calamity Jane's real name, and how did she earn her nickname?

6 What is South Dakota's state song?

7 When was the Dakota Territory created, and what future states were part of it?

8 On Mount Rushmore, how wide is Abraham Lincoln's mouth?

Words to Know

capitol: building for the legislature

commemorates: serves as a memorial or reminder

eroded: worn away over time by the action of water, wind, or glaciers

expedition: a journey made for exploration

fertile: able to easily sustain plant life

financial: having to do with money and business

frontier: land that forms the farthest part of a country's inhabited regions

heritage: a person's background

hydroelectric: electricity produced by using the power of flowing water

immigrants: people who left one country to live in another

mediums: materials or techniques that an artist chooses to use

nocturnal: active at night

pacifism: belief that the use of force is never justified

powwows: gatherings celebrating American Indian culture

receded: retreated, disappeared

reservations: lands set aside for American Indians

smelting: melting or fusing metals to lessen impure elements

till: glacial drift consisting of a mixture of clay, sand, gravel, and boulders

Index

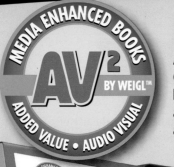

Log on to www.av2books.com

AV² by Weigl brings you media enhanced books that support active learning. Go to www.av2books.com, and enter the special code found on page 2 of this book. You will gain access to enriched and enhanced content that supplements and complements this book. Content includes video, audio, web links, quizzes, a slide show, and activities.

Audio
Listen to sections of the book read aloud.

Video
Watch informative video clips.

Embedded Weblinks
Gain additional information for research.

Try This!
Complete activities and hands-on experiments.

WHAT'S ONLINE?

Try This!	Embedded Weblinks	Video	EXTRA FEATURES
Test your knowledge of the state in a mapping activity.	Discover more attractions in South Dakota.	Watch a video introduction to South Dakota.	**Audio** Listen to sections of the book read aloud.
Find out more about precipitation in your city.	Learn more about the history of the state.	Watch a video about the features of the state.	
Plan what attractions you would like to visit in the state.	Learn the full lyrics of the state song.		**Key Words** Study vocabulary, and complete a matching word activity.
Learn more about the early natural resources of the state.			
Write a biography about a notable resident of South Dakota.			**Slide Show** View images and captions, and prepare a presentation.
Complete an educational census activity.			
			Quizzes Test your knowledge.

AV² was built to bridge the gap between print and digital. We encourage you to tell us what you like and what you want to see in the future.

Sign up to be an AV² Ambassador at www.av2books.com/ambassador.